WITHDRAWN

The Aquinas Lecture, 1966

THE PRAGMATIC MEANING OF GOD

Under the Auspices of the
Wisconsin-Alpha Chapter of Phi Sigma Tau

By

ROBERT O. JOHANN, S.J., PH.D.

MARQUETTE UNIVERSITY PRESS
MILWAUKEE
1966

Nihil Obstat

John A. Schulien, S.T.D., censor librorum
Milwaukiae, die 13 mensis Junis, 1966

Imprimatur

✝William E. Cousins
Archiepiscopus Milwaukiensis
Milwaukiae, die 5 Julie, 1966

Imprimi Potest

Very Rev. John J. McGinty S.J.
Provincial, New York Province
June 16, 1966

Second Printing—1967
Third Printing—1970

Library of Congress Catalog Number 66-26282

PRINTED
IN
U.S.A.

Prefatory

The Wisconsin-Alpha Chapter of Phi Sigma Tau, the National Honor Society for Philosophy at Marquette University, each year invites a scholar to deliver a lecture in honor of St. Thomas Aquinas whose feast day is March 7. These lectures are customarily given on the first or second Sunday of March.

The 1966 Aquinas Lecture "The Pragmatic Meaning of God" was delivered on March 6 in the Peter A. Brooks Memorial Union of Marquette University by Fr. Robert O. Johann, S.J., Associate Professor of Philosophy, Fordham University.

Fr. Johann was born in New York, in 1924. He earned the A.B. in 1947 and the M.A. in 1948 at St. Louis University. In 1953 he received the Ph.D. from Louvain University, Belgium.

He began his teaching career at the College of Philosophy and Letters, Fordham University in 1956. In 1963-64 he was Visiting Associate Professor of Philosophy at Yale University. The following year he became Associate Professor of Philosophy at Fordham University. From 1962-1966 he was Councillor of the Metaphysical Society of America.

Fr. Johann's publications include: *The Meaning of Love* (Westminster: Newman Press, 1955); "Experience and Philosophy," in *Experience, Existence, and the Good,* ed. I. C. Lieb (Southern Illinois University Press, 1961); "Teilhard's Personalized Universe," in *Teilhard Conference Proceedings* (Fordham, 1961); "Love and Justice," in *Ethics and Society,* ed. Richard T. De George (Garden City: Anchor Books, 1966); "Knowledge, Commitment and the Real," in *Wisdom in Depth,* ed. V. Daues, M. Halloway, L. Sweeney (Bruce Publishing Company, 1966); articles in *The Review of Metaphysics, Cross Currents, Thought,* and *America.*

To this list of publications Phi Sigma Tau is pleased to add: *The Pragmatic Meaning of God.*

The Pragmatic Meaning of God

Our aim is to discern anew the bearing or import of belief in God on the quality of our lives. Certain factors in contemporary life tend to obscure that import. Indeed, we have become so specialized in our interests and concerns that, for many, a question about the overall quality of life never even arises. Yet, as I shall try to show, it is central to the whole of philosophy. To give a certain order to my remarks, I have divided what follows into three sections. First, I shall examine the pervasive quality of life today. This, it is hoped, will disclose the reasons for the present eclipse of God. Secondly, I shall analyze the notion itself of "quality of life" in an effort to see what it involves and how to come to grips with it philosophically. Finally, an attempt will be made to spell out in some detail the way in which belief in God can enhance the quality of our own lives.

I

The present age is one in which the past is coming unstuck. Old attitudes, habits and ways of acting, valid and operative for centuries, no longer seem to be so. There is hardly a single area in our cultural and institutional life which is not being subjected to critical reappraisal. It is not surprising that, in a time of such general ferment, traditional ideas of religion and of God should be coming under attack. The mass media have made us all familiar with the paradoxical notions of a religionless Christianity and of a theology without God. But, although the fact of our changing attitudes and *mores* is manifest, the reasons underlying these changes are less so. At the outset, therefore, I would like to examine some of these reasons. For if our former pattern and way of life is breaking down, it is because it is no longer experienced as adequate. Something new is being disclosed on the level of experience which demands a new stance on our part, a new adjustment. If we feel dissatisfied with our present posture, it is because we feel at the same time that something else is required of us. What is it, then, that lies at the root of our present restlessness and dissatisfaction, and which is felt to be left out of account by our present ways of adjusting to the demands of reality?

Underlying and implicit in contemporary man's negative reaction to the past and to tradition is a new experiential awareness of himself, a new practical grasp of himself. Because this grasp has only begun to exert a distinctive influence, and because, moreover, it is manifested largely by way of opposition to what has gone before, it resists positive characterization. However, I think a few points can be made which may not only illumine its negativity with regard to present conditions, but also throw some light on specific future requirements.

Perhaps the dominant idea according to which contemporary man seeks to interpret his life is that of *creative interaction*. Contemporary man more and more views his life as a process of interaction (with environing physical and social forces) that is capable of generating ever new and richer meanings and is open to endless enhancement. Hence, the new and more thorough-going worldliness of his outlook. The world is not simply a point of passage on the way to fulfillment elsewhere. With all its resistances, efficacies and potentialities, it is the correlative pole of man's own energies and an essential part of the human. Man's fulfillment, therefore, is to be sought in the quality of the interactive process itself. This must be the focus of his effort and concern. As Dewey remarks: "Nothing but the best, the richest and fullest experience possible is good enough for man";[1] its attainment should be our "common purpose".

Together with this new secularity, however, note should also be taken of the new sense of personal transcendence involved in the contemporary outlook. Contemporary man sees himself as having a wider range of responsibility than heretofore.

1. John Dewey, *Experience and Nature* (New York: Dover, 1958), p. 412.

Not only has he emerged from the determinisms of psycho-physical nature;[2] he also transcends the whole realm of the determinate and matter-of-fact, including social structures, patterns and institutions.[3] He is responsible, therefore, not merely for conforming to pre-existing patterns but for the very shape of the patterns themselves. With a view to enhancing life's meaning and significance, facts must be changed as well as accepted. For contemporary man,

2. Cf. Max Scheler, *Man's Place in Nature,* trans. by Hans Meyerhoff (New York: Noonday, 1961), p. 39.

3. In speaking of man's transcendence of the determinate and matter of fact, our intention is not to introduce a kind of angelism that is alien to bodily life and its obvious limitations. Paul Ramsey, in his paper at the conference on "The Vatican Council and the World Today" held at Brown University on March 15, 1966, rightly criticizes such a view of freedom and responsibility as implying a new dualism. What we mean to insist upon is rather the creative role of intelligence, its capacity to move through facts to possibilities for genuine enhancement. This is simply another way of saying that the reasonable is what conforms, in the light of both facts and possibilities, to the requirements of reason; the reasonable is not defined by sheer conformity to the given.

therefore, nothing finite is final, nothing determinate is closed to improvement. Aware by his intelligence not only of facts but of possibilities, he exists in a true sense beyond limits and sees himself in the role of a perpetual and wholesale renovator.

Worldliness and personal transcendence, therefore, are closely interconnected. Instead of separating man from his environment, personal transcendence, as presently conceived, means a new intimacy and a more significant involvement with it. It marks the release of limitless possibilities and opens the door to a more truly human and genuinely *creative* participation of man in the world. Just as man's participation in the world would not be human at all without that minimal distance from things implied in man's *freedom to conform* to their structures, so the greater distance implied in the *freedom to innovate,* to alter and enhance the structures of experience, by the very fact that it enlarges reason's role, deepens the humanity of man's relationship to his environment. The greater man's distance from the world, i.e. the greater his relative transcendence, the more humanly is he joined to it. For this greater distance allows him to approach the world not only with appreciation and due regard for what it is, but with genuine care and creative concern for what it may become. It gives rise, therefore, to a new kind of wholeness —not that of a system or organism in which man has a fixed place that he is supposed, freely, to occupy, but the wholeness of an on-going encounter between independent initiatives, the wholeness of a continuing conversation which is at once a continuous challenge to inventive intelligence and a continuous consummation to the parties involved. Intelligent participation in this encounter is not only man's way to fulfillment; it is itself that fulfillment.

This deliberate assumption of creative responsibility for the shape of his life in the world, which is perhaps the most distinctive trait of contemporary man and dominates his outlook, issues in all sorts of consequences. For example, it is this,

I think, which lies behind much of his distrust for philosophy and religion. Before going into these areas, however, it may be well to examine a little just why it is that contemporary man finds this new stance so appealing.

The fundamental reason for contemporary man's fascination with the new ideal of creative responsibility and for his passionate rejection of any recommendations, no matter what their source, which do not do justice to it, is that it allows him to integrate his experience in a way never before possible. For what it gives promise of is precisely the restoration of man in his freedom and subjectivity to the world in which he finds himself. It overcomes the old division between the free subject and the determinate object. It allows man to belong to and participate in something other than himself and larger than himself in a way, nevertheless, that is proportionate to his creative energies. He can be party to something without being simply a part; belong to the other and still be himself.[4]

This is something new. Traditional outlooks are either dominantly objective or dominantly subjective in their orientation.[5] The "objective", for example, is empha-

4. The ideal of creative responsibility thus overcomes the limitations of the first two types of courage ("the courage to be as a part" and "the courage to be as oneself") described by Tillich as stages towards a final kind ("the courage to accept acceptance"), without its being identical with this final kind. Perhaps the courage implied in this new stance is more properly and simply "the courage to be human." Cf. Paul Tillich, *The Courage To Be* (New Haven: Yale Univ. Press, 1952).

5. Our remarks here are inspired by Francis H. Parker's perceptive article, "The Temporal Being of Western Man" (*Review of Metaphysics*, XVIII, No. 4, 629-646), in which he agrees with Erich Fromm that the fundamental challenge now confronting modern man is to achieve "a new relation of the free individual subject to the rest of reality." Parker is thinking of a philosophical synthesis that would combine the insights of pre-modern objectivism and modern subjectivism without their drawbacks, a synthesis he claims we do not yet have. What I am suggesting here is that contemporary experience, with its new emphasis on creative responsibility, is already providing a synthesis on the level of practice.

sized in ancient philosophy. Man is viewed primarily as one kind of being among other kinds. He is integrated with the world, not as a self, but as a determinate species among other determinate species. Characteristic of modern philosophy, on the other hand, is its emphasis on the subject. Whereas, in ancient philosophy, the world engulfs the self, in modern philosophy the tendency is for the self to engulf the world. Ancient philosophy allows little place for personal creativity. Modern philosophy all but takes the "response" out of responsibility. If ancient philosophy does not sufficiently take the self into account, modern philosophy, in taking it into account, practically eliminates the other.

In this respect, medieval philosophy is seen by many as a kind of hybrid that is finally no more adequate than what preceded it or followed it. Although under the influence of Christianity it does contain an emphasis on freedom, selfhood and personal destiny which is lacking in ancient philosophy, and although it has an idea of nature's radical and existential contingency which the ancients never had, still it brings the two together, self and nature, in a way that from the contemporary point of view is still unsatisfactory. For the world of medieval man still fails to provide a sufficient outlet for the critical, transforming and creative role of human intelligence. Medieval man is not sufficiently aware of temporal process and development. He is still too much inclined to view order in the world and in human institutions as a pre-supposition rather than as an accomplishment. Hence, for him, even though worldly order is contingent and does not have to be the way it is—indeed, does not have to be at all— still, it has been created the way it is by God and man's obligation as a creature of God is to conform to it. The purpose of rationality and intelligence, therefore, is free conformity rather than creativity. Man finds salvation by freely conforming to the intentions and will of God as manifested in the determinate structures of physical and social nature. He is integrated with the rest of creation, not precisely as a self, but rather as one who is also a creature.

From this we may gather the appeal of the new stance and outlook. It manages to combine the realism of ancient and medieval philosophy with the creativity of modern philosophy. Unlike modern philosophy, it does not leave man a lonely ego, but involves him dramatically in a real, objective world that transcends him. This world of contemporary man, however, is one that invites intervention. It presents itself as a challenge to the full range of his inventive powers. It evokes all the energies of man's imagination and intelligence to contribute to its own transformation and enhancement. The world, therefore, is viewed not as hostile to human creativity, either inherently or by God's intent, but precisely as the field for its deployment. This is the new integrity which the contemporary stance provides for human experience. Man feels himself to be humanly and creatively one with his environment in a way that he has never felt before.

Such oneness, of course, does not mean an absence of problems. The problematic and the uncertain, along with the anxieties they produce, all but obsess contemporary man. In a sense, man has never felt less secure than he does now. But, however much the man of today may be nostalgic for a simpler past, he not only knows he cannot return to it but is resolutely set against any such effort. For he feels that at last he has come of age as a responsible being with a task, here and now set him, that is fully proportionate to the whole scope of his personal capacities.

With this in mind, we can perhaps better understand contemporary man's negative attitude toward philosophy and religion, and his positive love affair with science. Philosophy fails to excite him because it has separated itself from the focus of his interests. Too long philosophy has viewed itself as supplying man with access to the really real, a realm that is somehow behind or above experience and feudally superior to it. As Josef Peiper once put it, philosophy represents man's stepping out of the workaday world into a contemplative position face to face with the Whole.[6] But this is precisely what contemporary man does not want. He does not want to step out of the workaday world but to enhance it. Nor is he interested merely in contemplating reality but is bent instead on rendering it more humanly meaningful and significant.

The same can be said for philosophy's traditional pursuit of necessary truths and underlying conditions of possibility. Contemporary man is simply not interested in a systematic study of the permanent and necessary structure of being. What is permanent and necessary, he feels, will be as it is regardless of whether or not man attends to it. What contemporary man wants to know is precisely those variables that affect his situation here and now, and which can be so modified as to bring about a general improvement of the human condition. Hence, his fascination with science. For science is concerned, not with the

6.   Josef Pieper, *Leisure the Basis of Culture* (New York: Pantheon, 1952), p. 122.

fixed, but with the variable. It is interested in corollating change with change, changes going on here with changes going on elsewhere, so that man may be provided with a measure of control and direction over what happens in his world. Thus we are beginning to hear, even from Catholic writers, that we must temper our passion for ultimate meanings, let go our preoccupation with philosophy and theology, even our efforts to construct new philosophies and new theologies, and busy ourselves with the physical and social sciences if we are going to catch up with our world.[7]

The integral "this-worldliness" of the contemporary mind also lies behind the contemporary rejection of religion. As one writer expresses it: "The epoch whose ethos is quickly spreading into every corner of the globe is an age of 'no religion at all'. It no longer looks to religious rules

7. See, for example, Daniel Callahan, "The Secular City: Toward a Theology of Secularity," *Commonweal*, LXXXII, No. 21 (Sept. 17, 1965), pp. 658-662.

and rituals for its morality or its meanings."[8] In other words, contemporary man finds that being in the world makes sense without God. This was not the case so long as the world could not provide scope for personal creativity, but called instead for conformity. As long as it was considered necessary simply to accept things the way they were, God provided a motive for doing so. Conforming to the *status quo,* however contingent it was recognized to be, was viewed as conforming to God's will. Since there was no place for creative intervention on the part of the individual with regard to the given patterns and structures of this world, it was *in his relationship to God,* not in his relationship to the world, that the individual person found his final meaning and fulfillment.

But a world conceived as beckoning to be transformed, and transformed by man's own intelligence, is one which does not need God for man's place in it to make sense. Such a world, by the very fact that

8. Harvey Cox, *The Secular City* (New York: Macmillan, 1965), p. 3.

it provides an outlet equal to man's powers, offers itself as the place of his fulfillment. God may still be necessary to account for the world's and man's existence. He is not, however, a factor in their mutual and harmonious fit. Indeed, He is not even needed as a motive for personal dedication. Once man realizes that his vocation is to intervene creatively in his environment for the achievement of a more truly human life, he finds the goods already present in experience sufficiently attractive to inspire his efforts to secure and extend them.[9] Is not this the chief source of embarrassment for religious people today? They find those who profess no religion at all even more energetic than themselves in working for social justice and the achievement of a better life for mankind.

But God and religion are more than irrelevant to man's vocation; preoccupation with them also prevents its achievement. To situate man's goal beyond and outside this world reduces the present

9. Cf. John Dewey, *A Common Faith* (New Haven: Yale Univ. Press, 1934), pp. 70-73.

scene to a passing phase and encourages passivity regarding its shortcomings rather than active concern. One cannot serve two Masters. If the point of life lies outside life itself, how work wholeheartedly for life's enhancement? Moreover, the idea that eternal salvation is to be reached only through certain institutional channels, by discouraging individual and critical discernment, retards the development of the very skills needed for coping with this world. Religion is thus felt to be prolonging man's childhood instead of helping him to come of age. Indeed, the particularism of its institutional forms reduces mankind to quarreling children, divided from one another in their deepest concerns and unable to work together.

It will be noted that, as we have presented them, these criticisms all form a piece, a logical whole. The logic, however, is not speculative and abstract, but concrete. In other words, Godlessness today is not the conclusion of a syllogism which starts out from the Sartrean premise: there is no God. Nor do I think it the case that the Godless man arises primarily from a decision to ignore God.[10] The whole point of our remarks so far is that contemporary man's negative attitude toward God and religion has its roots in a new and positive awareness of himself. Contemporary man is not so much anti-theistic as he is pro-human. His present experience has provided him with a new sense and feel for the human, with which the notion of God embodied in traditional religions seems at loggerheads.[11]

What we are dealing with, therefore, is not primarily a philosophy. It is really a new way of life—one whose implications and exigencies are only beginning to be grasped reflectively. The unifying focus of this new style is the challenge to intelligence inherent in the experiential process itself.[12] The resultant sense of creative re-

10. John C. Murray, S.J., on the contrary, would seem to hold for such a decision. See his "On the Structure of the Problem of God," *Theological Studies* XXIII, No. 1, 1-26.
11. Cf. A. Dondeyne, "Les leçons positives de l'athéisme contemporain," *Il Problema dell' Ateismo* (Brescia, 1962).
12. Cf. John Dewey, *A Common Faith*, p. 79.

sponsibility gives contemporary experience its distinctive and integrating quality, which is felt to be sufficient without God. Today's Godlessness, then, springs neither from theory nor choice, but from the felt discrepancy between our theological images and the concrete quality of our lives. Since this notion of "quality of life" is central to our thesis, a more detailed analysis of it is called for.

II

The notion of quality, as we are using it, is not unlike the classic notion of form. As Tillich puts it, "Everything real has a form, be it an atom, be it the human mind. That which has no form has no being."[13] Form is that by which a given thing is the sort of thing it is. It is the characteristic way the different members of a complex reality are related to one another. In this sense, quality or form is not a property which something possesses in addition to its other properties; it is the distinctive

13. Paul Tillich, *Love, Power, and Justice* (London: Oxford Univ. Press, 1954), p. 54.

property of the whole, pervading all its members as the very manner in which they are conjoined. Thus, for example, we may speak of a painting as having a Rembrandt quality. This would not be a particular feature of the painting alongside other features. Rather, it would be something "which externally demarcates it from other paintings and which internally pervades, colors, tones, and weights every detail and every relation of the work" in question.[14]

What is distinctive, however, about our use of the notion of quality stems from that to which we are applying it. For we are not conceiving quality or form as a principle inherent in things taken separately and identical with their individual natures. We are applying the notion to the interaction between things, or more precisely, to the interaction between the human self and its environment. In other words, life—in the phrase "quality of life"

14. John Dewey, "Qualitative Thought," reprinted in *John Dewey on Experience, Nature, and Freedom*, ed. by Richard J. Bernstein (New York: Liberal Press, 1960), p. 179.

—is being restricted to the life of a human subject, the human self. Moreover, this life is not to be conceived merely as something going on within the human self, something essentially private and subjective. Since it is the very interaction between self and other, it includes within itself as essential and dynamically interrelated components both the human person and the whole range of its environment.

Life here, therefore, is very similar to Dewey's notion of experience. Remarking that William James called experience a double-barreled word, Dewey goes on to comment:

> "Experience" denotes the planted field, the sowed seeds, the reaped harvests, the changes of night and day, spring and autumn, wet and dry, heat and cold that are observed, feared, longed for; it also denotes the one who plants and reaps, who works and rejoices, hopes, fears, plans, invokes magical chemistry to aid him, who is downcast or triumphant. It is "double-barreled" in that it recognizes in its primary integrity no division between act and material, subject and object, but

contains them both in an unanalyzed totality.[15]

This totality is, moreover, all-embracing. It includes not only all the things with which we directly deal, but also whatever is in any way connected with those things. Nothing at all is excluded. A person's life, therefore, is in a sense the whole of reality.[16] Not everything, to be sure, is contained there *mente*—we are certainly not explicitly and distinctly aware of all the factors ingredient in our experience and having a bearing on its outcome—but, as Blondel observes, everything is involved *facto*.[17] Indeed, the aim of all thoughtful inquiry is precisely to reduce this discrepancy. Only in the measure that we discriminate the factors actually functioning within our experience and determine the bearing of each on what we undergo, does

15. John Dewey, *Experience and Nature*, p. 8.
16. For a fuller treatment of this point, see my "The Return to Experience," *Review of Metaphysics*, XVII, No. 3, 319-339, esp. pp. 325-6.
17. Maurice Blondel, "Le point de départ de la recherche philosophique," *Annales de Philosophie Chrétienne* (Avril-Septembre 1906), p. 240.

the shape of our lives begin to come under our own direction and control.

In identifying human life and reality in this way we are led to the idea that there are, in a sense, as many universes of the real as there are persons. The very plurality of persons involves a kind of multiplication of reality. But as André Marc has observed, the real does not multiply and share itself with distinct individuals except to recover and find itself whole again in the life of each.[18] In other words, the multiplication that takes place is more a multiplication of perspectives. The same universe is lived by each person from his own point of view. In the dynamic synthesis between himself and all the rest, which is identically each person's life, he is the only one that functions as "I". Thus each person is, in a sense, entitled to speak of the totality of the real as "my" life, "my" experience. But if this all-embracing whole is lived by each person from his own point of view, so that it becomes identically his

18. André Marc, *Raison et conversion chrétienne* (Paris: Desclée de Brouwer, 1961), p. 20.

life, it does not thereby cease to be the one real in which all communicate and by which all are encompassed.

Now it is to this total reality, but conceived precisely as one with any person's life, that we are applying the notion of quality. "Quality of life" will not be a property or feature belonging to any particular element within experience, but will characterize the interactive process itself. As expressed, it will designate the sort of process that is going on, the characteristic way in which all the multiple elements ingredient in the process are conjoined. And since this process is both life and reality, the quality of a person's life will also be the quality of the real itself—the sort of sense it makes or fails to make, the sort of unity it has or fails to have, depending on the particular way the person in question goes about relating himself to his overall environment.[19]

19. For a treatment of the bearing of one's personal orientation on the final sense of reality, see my "Knowledge, Commitment and the Real," *Wisdom in Depth*, ed. by V. Daues, M. Hollo-

This notion of quality can perhaps be made clearer if we see the use to which John Dewey puts it to distinguish from the general flow of experience at large those episodes in life that stand out as singular and distinct experiences.

As Dewey points out, philosophers are given to talking for the most part about experience in general, whereas idiomatic speech just as commonly refers to particular experiences, each having its own beginning and end.[20] *An* experience, as distinct from experience at large, has a certain unity and coherence about it. Dewey writes:

> . . . We have an experience when the material experienced runs its course to fulfillment. Then and then only is it integrated within and demarcated in the general stream of experience from other experiences. A piece of work is finished in a way that is satisfactory; a problem receives its solution; a game is played

19.　(Cont.) way, L. Sweeney (Milwaukee: Bruce, 1966), pp. 112-125.
20.　John Dewey, *Art as Experience* (New York: Minton, Balch & Co., 1934), p. 35.

through; a situation, whether that of eating a meal, playing a game of chess, carrying on a conversation, writing a book, or taking part in a political campaign, is so rounded out that its close is a consummation and not a cessation. Such an experience is a whole, and carries with it its own individualizing quality and self-sufficiency.[21]

Not all of our experience is of this kind. As Dewey remarks in another place:

. . . In much of our experience we are not concerned with the connection of one incident with what went before and what comes after. There is no interest that controls attentive rejection or selection of what shall be organized into the developing experience. Things happen, but they are neither definitely included nor decisively excluded; we drift. We yield according to external pressure, or evade and compromise. There are beginnings and cessations, but no genuine initiations and concludings. One thing replaces another, but does not absorb it and carry it on. There is experience, but so slack and discursive that it is not *an* experience.[22]

21. *Ibid.*
22. *Ibid.*, p. 40.

The difference between these two sorts of experience may be summed up by characterizing them as in the one case having, and in the other case lacking, esthetic quality. What sets off *an* experience is its pattern, structure, its quality of making complete sense. All the phases that can be discriminated within it are nevertheless grasped in their interconnections and seen as contributing to the final outcome. There is no intimation of anything to be added as required for its completion, no suggestion of superfluous elements that could be removed without distorting it. Like a work of art, it is a harmonious whole, satisfying for contemplation just as it stands.

But this esthetic quality is precisely what life taken as a whole too often seems to lack. However much our individual lives may be graced at intervals with esthetic episodes, these are too intermittent and sporadic, too much like widely separated oases in a wasteland of irrelevant impressions and incoherent details, to add up to anything in particular. In fact, the esthetic is such a rare occurence in our lives and comes always as such a happy surprise, that we are almost inevitably inclined to think of it as some kind of benign visitation from another, higher world rather than as in any way normative for our experience in this one. In contrast to these grace-filled moments, the quality of our lives as a whole is too often anesthetic.

Now it is my contention that the relatively anesthetic quality of our experience in general constitutes the central philosophical problem. This is to say that the ultimate aim of philosophy as a human undertaking is the enhancement of life's quality and that the final criterion for its meaningfulness is the measure in which it makes such enhancement possible. However theoretical it may be in its own immediate nature, it is only as involved in this larger task of reshaping and restructuring experience along esthetic lines—only as contributing to the emergence of esthetic quality in life at large so that the whole of life becomes enjoyable in its very wholeness, coherence and concrete reasonableness—it is only thus, I say, that philosophy has any final worth or significance.

Needless to say, this idea that philosophy is not its own end, that its goal, like that of all meaningful thought, is fundamentally practical—not practical in the sense of being subordinated to some particular aim within life, but as looking to the general enhancement of practice itself, the constitution of life at large on an ever higher level of meaning and coherence—has not always been recognized. Instead of being seen as a tool and method for the general reconstruction of experience, philosophy has too often been taken as providing some kind of escape or refuge from experience.

To a certain extent this was inevitable. On the level of intellectual interpretation, it was the natural fruit of a situation which lacked modern science and technology. So long as man, through lack of scientific knowledge, was unable to alter significantly the shape and quality of his life, there was really nothing for him to do but leave it pretty much as it was and look for fulfillment elsewhere. Philosophy itself gave promise of such fulfillment. In contrast to the realm of everyday experience which, whatever its inherent satisfactions, was always a matter of loose ends and left-overs, of broken promises and dashed hopes, philosophy provided access to a secure realm of eternal and changeless essences where everything was neatly tucked in and squared away. The certainty and necessity of its objects furnished compensation for the uncertain and haphazard quality of everyday life. But this compensation came at a price that we are still paying. It meant the separation of philosophy from concrete, practical issues, from having any share in shaping the course of life. If people today have little regard for the possible contribution of philosophy to the achievement of a better world, it is because philosophy itself has long held the view that this is not its task. By centering on the "really real," it forgot the world in which men live.

When we say that life itself provides philosophy with its central problem, it is

not our intention to suggest that the problem of life can be resolved by thought
alone. Thinking apart from action modifies
nothing and hence can resolve nothing.
As Dewey remarks: "Some decisive action
is needed in order to establish contact with
the realities of the world and in order that
impressions may be so related to facts that
their value is tested and organized."[23] But
if thought by itself is unable to enhance
life's concrete quality, mere action is even
less equipped to do so.

> Zeal for doing, lust for action, leaves
> many a person, especially in this hurried
> and impatient human environment in
> which we live, with experience of an al-
> most incredible paucity, all on the sur-
> face. No one experience has a chance to
> complete itself because something else is
> entered upon so speedily. What is called
> experience becomes so dispersed and mis-
> cellaneous as hardly to deserve the name.
> Resistance is treated as an obstruction to
> be beaten down, not as an invitation to
> reflection. An individual comes to seek,

23.   *Ibid.*, p. 45.

> unconsciously even more than by deliberate choice, situations in which he can do the most things in the shortest time.[24]

In other words, if disembodied thought is impotent to affect change, "action, which is not informed with vision, imagination, and reflection, is more likely to increase confusion and conflict than to straighten things out."[25] What is needed, therefore, is a happy and fruitful combination of the two—an action that is open and submissive to the direction and control of thought, and a thought that is concerned with the problem itself of action.[26]

To be concerned with the problem of action, however, is to be concerned with more than the mere discovery of ever more efficacious means to preconceived ends. It is to be concerned with those ends

24. *Ibid.*, pp. 44-45.
25. John Dewey, *Creative Intelligence: Essays in the Pragmatic Attitude* (New York: Henry Holt & Co., 1917), p. 65.
26. Cf. M. Blondel, *op. cit.*, pp. 226-227; also Section V of Dewey's "The Need for a Recovery of Philosophy" in *Creative Intelligence*, pp. 53-69.

themselves and their interrelation.[27] This is a mistake of many of our contemporaries (including Catholics) who are insisting that in order to catch up with our world we should forego the pursuit of "ultimate meaning" and concentrate our attention on the findings of economics, sociology and political science. The reason behind this suggestion is clear enough. "Ultimate meaning" is still confused in their minds with that realm of the really real that we have rejected.

But such is clearly not the only signi-

27. "As a matter of fact, the pragmatic theory of intelligence means that the function of mind is to project new and more complex ends—to free experience from routine and from caprice. Not the use of thought to accomplish purposes already given either in the mechanism of the body or in that of the existent state of society, but the use of intelligence to liberate and liberalize action, is the pragmatic lesson" (Dewey, *Creative Intelligence*, p. 63). Cf. also J. Macmurray, *The Self as Agent* (New York: Harper, 1957), p. 23, where he writes: "The essential reference of theoretical to practical activities does not involve the control of theory by practice. It consists even more significantly in the control of practice by theory; in the determination, through reflection, of the ends of action."

ficance that can be attached to the term.
For even after we have explored and made
our own all the meaningful connections
and corollations between elements and objects in our experience, such as science dis-
closes them to be, there always remains
the further question as to the bearing of
all these findings on the quality of our
lives. When we have amassed all the facts,
we still have to ask ourselves what we are
to do with them. No matter how much we
may wish to avoid it, the question of valu-
ation and of establishing some priority of
values imposes itself upon us. And this,
I suggest, is a meaning of "ultimate meaning" which we cannot ignore no matter
how hard-headed and practical we want
to become. We cannot preach the enhancement of experience or the bettering
of mankind's lot unless we have some idea
of what such improvement consists in.
Such an idea, however, is the fruit, not of
scientific inquiry in the strict sense, but
rather of philosophical investigation and
reflection. No small part of our trouble
today stems from the fact that this reflec-

tion proceeds haphazardly and in an undisciplined manner with those who are engaged in it not even aware of what they are doing.

There are, I would say, two fundamental tasks for the philosopher who would cast in his lot with struggling humanity and strive to make his philosophy relevant to human affairs. The two tasks are closely interrelated and actually condition one another. The first is, in the light of all the available facts and the possibilities inherent in them, to determine in a tentative way a comprehensive ideal of human action. To what sort of wholeness are men called? To what kind of inclusive coherence do they aspire? Such a determination is fundamentally esthetic in character. It tries to envision not abstractly, but in the light of existing conditions, an ideal of comprehensive satisfactoriness.[28] It is

28. The "comprehensively satisfactory" for a rational being, whose nature it is to respond to the *rationes* of things, cannot be anything that, in the light of intelligence, fails to meet the objective requirements of his situation. What has to be envisioned is how these requirements can be fitted together into a harmonious whole.

necessarily tentative and open-ended, because it is a work of constructive interpretation whose adequacy can never be internally guaranteed. But it is nonetheless a necessary enterprise if the process of specific evaluation is to go on at all. For we cannot speak of the bearing of some specific belief, practice, or procedure on the quality of human life without presupposing some idea of the shape which that life ought to have.

The second and abiding task of the philosopher, and one moreover which must go on simultaneously with the first, is the work of constant and universal criticism. At any given time, the actual shape of our lives, their relatively anesthetic quality, is the fruit of all sorts of beliefs and practices which we have inherited from the past but whose connections with what we actually undergo have never been brought to light. These beliefs and practices implicitly contain broad interpretations of life and of the world. In themselves, and in their institutional embodiments, they represent our large scale adjustment to reality. They go to make up the broad cultural context out of which we operate in our pursuit of particular objectives. But this context, since it is presupposed by those strivings which preoccupy us and hold our attention, tends itself to go unnoticed and unquestioned. Although pervading the meaning of all that we do, it is taken for granted. Its unexamined character, however, does not prevent it, as I say, from having important and fateful consequences. Our concrete grasp of the sense and shape of life itself is largely the function of these implicit and habitual interpretations.

Now it is these large-scale interpretations and attitudes, implicitly operative in all that we do, that constitute, as Dewey remarks,

> . . . the *immediate* primary material of philosophical reflection. The aim of the latter is to criticize this material, to clarify it, to organize it, to test its internal coherence and to make explicit its consequences.[29]

29. John Dewey, "Context and Thought," in *John Dewey on Experience, Nature, and Freedom,* p. 106.

Or again:

> Philosophy is criticism, criticism of
> the influential beliefs that underlie
> culture; a criticism which traces the be-
> liefs to their generating conditions as far
> as may be, which tracks them to their re-
> sults, which considers the mutual com-
> patibility of the elements, of the total
> structure of beliefs. Such an examination
> terminates, whether so intended or not,
> in a projection of them into a new per-
> spective which leads to new surveys of
> possibilities.[30]

This last phrase indicates the connection
between this second work of philosophy,
that of criticism, with its first work indicated above, that, namely, of esthetic con-
struction. In other words, the aim of the
work of criticism is to determine the bearing of these influential beliefs and attitudes on the quality of our life as a whole,
i.e. to determine not only what positive
contributions they make, but also how they
may in particular instances constrict and
diminish life's humanness. The two phases
of philosophical reflection thus go hand

30. *Ibid.*, p. 107.

in hand. The lack of coherence of particular beliefs with the projected ideal provides the basis, once this incoherence is remarked, for the re-thinking of particular beliefs. The re-evaluation of particular beliefs, on the other hand, since these concern the elements which the ideal orders and integrates, allows for the reformation of the ideal and the projection of a more adequate one.

III

As already suggested, the incoherence of theological images with the concrete shape of life today is what lies behind much of the contemporary rejection of religion. When people say today that talk of God is meaningless and irrelevant, what they mean is that traditional religious beliefs and practices are no longer determining the actual quality of contemporary life. Not only are they not felt to enhance that quality; they really have nothing to do with it. In the measure, therefore, they are still entertained, they cannot but be experienced as so much excess baggage.

The honest and practical thing to do is to cut loose from them.[31]

Pragmatic considerations of this sort are characteristic of the contemporary mind. The difficulty, however, is that they manifest small regard for method. There has been little or no attempt to spell out, even tentatively, a contemporary ideal of humanness. The ultimacy of contemporary man's general orientation, his this-worldliness, with which traditional beliefs are in conflict, is taken for granted. And these beliefs, instead of being subjected to any kind of searching and discriminating criticism, are simply being rejected because of that conflict. Because the cultivation of God has not succeeded in humanizing man completely, indeed because it has had obvious negative consequences on this process of humanization—separating man from his world, dividing him from his fellows, introducing a kind of split between

31. It is interesting to note the similarity of these sentiments, which appear throughout Dewey's *A Common Faith*, written in 1934, with those of the very recent literature on "the death of God."

the human and the spiritual within man himself—it should be dropped altogether. According to Dewey, a piety towards man's inventive intelligence should *replace* the traditional and historic piety towards a a transcendent God. A kind of religious humanism, i.e. a whole-hearted devotion to human values conceived in exclusive terms, can do the job of traditional religion without its drawbacks.[32] Implicit and presupposed in all this is a kind of essential opposition between the human and the divine. Because God is Other, He must be alien. Because the human is self-sufficient, God must be an intruder.

It is this presupposition that I want to question. The purpose of what follows is to show not only how God is intrinsically constitutive of the human, but how explicit and thematic attention to Him alone makes possible the full realization of the human. In other words, granting the failures and

32. "One of the few experiments in the attachment of emotion to ends that mankind has not tried is that of devotion, so intense as to be religious, to intelligence as a force in social action" (*A Common Faith,* p. 79).

shortcomings of traditional religious ori-
entations, one can still maintain that these
are accidental rather than essential. The
task confronting us today, then, is not one
of building a world from which God is
deliberately excluded. It is rather a work
of criticism, of rethinking and purifying
our notions of both God and religion, so
that their influence on our lives, far from
being distorting, can be seen as wholly
constructive.

In order to show this, I propose to pro-
ceed in three steps. The first step will consist in sketching out a conception of the
ideal. I shall try to point out what that
wholeness is to which we aspire in all our
actions. The second step will indicate the
positive bearing of belief in God on the
realization of this ideal. For, not only is
an idea of God implicit in the ideal; the
ideal itself cannot be realized without explicit attention being paid to Him. Thirdly,
since the ideal embraces every dimension
of our lives, I shall try to spell out some
possible effects of religious belief on these
various dimensions. My purpose will be to

clarify how belief in God, instead of being a force for alienation, is actually what restores us to our neighbor, to ourselves, and to our world.

To construct an ideal of human action is to indicate what is required for a person's life to have maximum coherence. A person's life, we have said, is the continuous interaction between himself and the whole range of the other. The quality of this life, the quality of personal experience, will consist in the sort of relations that prevail between the self and the other.

Now, the first prerequisite, if this quality is to be characterized as one of wholeness or coherence, is that these relationships be basically interpersonal. The reason is clear. For the impersonal is by definition that which leaves the person out of account, that which is indifferent to and exclusive of the person. If, then, the other to which the self is related, were wholly impersonal in being and behavior, the self would be radically isolated, shut off from union and wholeness. Indeed, apart from another who awaits the self's response, the very capacity to give such a response, i.e. one's very selfhood, becomes meaningless.[33]

More, however, is needed if the interaction between self and other is to be qualified by wholeness. The merely personal nature of the other is not yet sufficient. For example, were self and other related only in terms of cooperation in the pursuit of some particular objective which each one desires on the basis of self-interest and yet cannot secure without the other's help, then the relationship prevailing between them would still be more functional than personal. They would be related to one another in terms of their respective contributions to the common enterprise, not in terms of themselves.[34] Hence the selfhood of each would be left on the margin of the unity established. Only when I am responsive to a personal other who is turned towards me and gives

33. See my "Knowledge, Commitment, and the Real," *Wisdom in Depth*, pp. 117-118.
34. Cf. John Macmurray, *Persons in Relation* (New York: Harper, 1961), p. 186.

me access to his very life and reality as a person, that is to say, only when the relationship between us is one of mutual responsiveness to one another as persons, is wholeness achieved. This, of course, is the exciting and satisfying thing about personal love and friendship. It gives us an experiential taste of that wholeness to which as persons we are called.

However, a friendship between myself and one or other person does not yet constitute my life as wholly satisfactory. For the personal other within whose love I seek inclusion is not made up of one or other person; it breaks down into an indefinite multitude of persons. Unless, therefore, you and I are lovingly related to these other persons who are actively part of our lives and determinants of its shape, our own friendship, instead of being a kind of final fulfillment, will be experienced as a minor mutuality constantly threatened and on the defensive against a potentially hostile environment. Instead of wholeness and harmony, it will be the divisions and antagonisms born of fear that

will characterize our lives. The kind of
wholeness, therefore, to which we as persons aspire, the ideal towards which our
actions as rational are implicitly directed,
is a wholeness of universal fellowship. It
is a universal community of persons each
of whom is lovingly disposed towards
every other. Only the achievement of such
a community can make our lives fully
whole.[35]

Such an ideal, admittedly, sounds uto-
pian. Lest we be put off at the outset by
this, a word of explanation is called for.
In the first place, it should be remarked
that this ideal is not, as it were, cut from
whole cloth. Universal community is not
an imaginatively constructed ideal that is
unrelated to goods and values we actually
experience. On the contrary, it is simply
the extension of something we not only
enjoy, but know to be that without which
we could not even begin to function as
persons. Indeed, it is precisely because we

35. Cf. the whole chapter, "The Celebration of
     Communion," in Macmurray's *Persons in Rela-
     tion,* but especially pp. 159-165.

find this essential value threatened by its partial realization, by the fact that it does not actually function universally, that we are pushed to extend its range.

Secondly, to proclaim universal community as the ideal is not to imply that it can be realized overnight, or even within the confines of historical time. Having a goal is not useless simply because it can never be fully realized. As we pointed out above, the whole work of evaluating specific beliefs and practices presupposes that we have at least tentatively determined an ideal of comprehensive satisfactoriness. Moreover, to reject the ideal merely because it is an ideal, not to take steps to extend fellowship because the fruit of all our efforts will always be limited in scope, would be to undermine that degree of community which has already been achieved. For community is not a settled fact. It is a matter of intention. It depends on the abiding intention of each of the members to behave reasonably and responsibly, i.e. lovingly, towards the others, to work continuously for a coherent order of harmonious relations. In other words, it requires on the part of each an unselfish concern for others, a will to promote wholeness. But to will wholeness in a limited way is not to will it at all. It is to settle for an overall orientation of opposition and conflict which makes self-interest primary and so corrupts all personal community at its root.[36]

If we accept the ideal of universal community as a required extension of that which makes life human and personal in the first place, our next step must be to explore the conditions presupposed for its effective pursuit. We have already indicated our conviction that explicit belief in God is such a condition. Why is this so?

Any unity of persons as persons in-

36. ". . . The inherent ideal of the personal . . . is a universal community of persons in which each cares for all the others and no one for himself. This ideal of the personal is also the condition of freedom—that is, of a full realization of his capacity to act—for every person. Short of this there is unintegrated, and therefore suppressed, negative motivation; there is unresolved fear; and fear inhibits action and destroys freedom" (Macmurray, *Persons in Relation*, p. 159).

volves *personal response* to an intention of unity. This notion of response is important. I can decide to love another (in the sense of being devoted to his welfare) regardless of his attitude towards me. I cannot, however, simply decide on my own to be friends with him. Friendship, as a mutual relationship, must be mutually intended.[37] If the other is uninterested or for any reason does not intend the union, no efforts on my part will be enough to constitute it. Our friendship can become a reality only in the measure each of us is *responsive to an intention of unity on the part of the other.*

What is true here of friendship is true of any personal community. Participation in such a union is achieved only through an individual's responsiveness to the will of another intending that relationship. But there is this difference. When the relationship of personal community is not restricted to pairs of individuals but extends to an indefinite plurality of persons, there

37.   Recall the remark of St. Thomas: "Amicus est amico amicus" (*Summa Theologica* II-II, 23, 1c).

must be one to whom all are responsive. I do not become a member of a community by entering into a personal union with one or other of its members, nor even with all of them taken separately. I become a member only by responding to that other who by being in reciprocal relation with every member of the group, is the source of their unity. He is one who intends each of them (and me too), not in isolation nor in relation only to himself, but precisely as related to the others, and his intention of unity, as already responsively recognized by the plurality, is precisely what makes it a community instead of a mere collection.

In other words, personal community among many individuals implies a personal head, through responsiveness to whom each of the individuals enters into responsive relationship with all the others.[38] Without a personal head, whose

38. Cf. Teilhard de Chardin, *The Phenomenon of Man* (New York: Harper, 1959), p. 267. It should be noted that the head of a personal community, a unity of persons *as persons,* cannot be conceived merely in organic terms. This is

intention of unity for the many is commonly—and in common—recognized by

not to say that personal fellowship or community can dispense with organizational structure. It is not a purely inward reality, but is located in space and time. It must be capable of co-ordinated, directed action to be able to meet the challenges and demands which the environment places on it, and to provide itself with the conditions for its own life as a community of persons. A community of persons, therefore, if it is to survive, requires organizational unity. Such a unity, however, is functional. Although it is needed for the external embodiment of community, it is not by itself enough to constitute it. The unity which structure or organization engenders is that of a whole made up of parts in which each has its place and in which all conspire for the procurement of a satisfactory relationship with environing conditions. But the community of persons is a whole made up of wholes. It unites persons, not in terms of functions and capacities, but rather in terms of what is deepest and most personal in themselves; in terms of their very reality as persons. That is why Teilhard is right, I think, in conceiving the authority or headship required for personal community as a transcendent source of personal love. It must be personal and loving, because only such a principle is able to attain the plurality of persons in their reality as persons. And since it reaches out universally to all persons, and grounds the unity of the whole inter-personal order, it must itself be transcendent.

them, there is no personal community. Hence, just as the achievement of friendship requires initiative on the side of the other, so also here. One can no more achieve personal community by going around loving everybody than one can achieve friendship simply on one's own. However, whereas the other, whose initiative is required in the case of friendship, is one among the many and on equal footing with them, the other needed for community is a principle (of unity) for the many, a kind of universal focus. Thus, if community implies headship (authority), headship always involves a measure of transcendence.

What this means for the problem confronting us is clear. If man's personal nature orients him towards the ideal of universal personal community, a universal fellowship of persons, it must at the same time situate him in a relation of responsibility towards a transcendent ground and universal focus of the whole interpersonal order. The very idea of universal community involves the idea of an already

existing Other who is in a position of headship (authority) over all persons, such
that actual responsiveness to Him actually
unites them to one another as persons. Indeed, it implies that even prior to the
achievement of personal community, men
are already in an ontological relationship
of common responsibility, that to be a
person is to be in *moral solidarity* with
other persons, called to answer the same
Transcendent Initiative.

Now, such a Universal Initiative, con-
stitutively present and correlative to every
self, the unifying ground or "head" of the
whole order of persons, the Person of persons (in Scheler's phrase), whose intention is the unity of all our intentions, i.e.
the realization of genuine and universal
community, is, I suggest, God. God and
the community of persons go together. Not
only can I not think universal community
without thinking God; I cannot effectively
intend such community without intending
responsiveness to Him. For, as we have
seen, membership in community demands
conscious conjunction with others in com-

mon recognition of, and response to, the authoritative intention of community. Unless members of a community are jointly aware of their unity with one another through their allegiance to a common head, they simply are not members and there is no community. To aim at a universal community of persons, therefore, is to aim at a universal responsiveness to God.

God, then, is not to be conceived the way Dewey maintains He is traditionally, i.e. as the antecedent realization of the ideal. Dewey sees the traditional concept of God as a kind of imaginative projection of the ideal into the order of actuality.[39] It is as if people were constrained to think of the ideal as actual in order to give it solidity and the ability to mobilize their energies. But the ideal is neither actual nor is it God. The ideal is the unification of men as persons. God is not that unification, but the Transcendent Initiative whose intention makes it possible. It is because

39.   Cf. *A Common Faith*, p. 49.

each person is constituted a person by being in a relationship of responsibility towards God that the plurality of persons is able to share the exercise of that responsibility and form itself into a community of persons.

The bearing of religion and belief in God on the social dimension of our lives, on our relationship with one another, is therefore clear. Cultivation of the divine is not a force of alienation but a source of unification. If this has not always worked out historically, if religion in practice has all too often turned out to be a divisive factor among men, the fault does not lie in the fact that men have believed in God. It is because they have confused the Transcendent with their own limited and particular representations of Him.[40] Men need

40. Another confusion undermining the pragmatic meaning of belief is that between organizational authority and personal authority. Since the common life of fellowship needed embodiment in an organization if it was to survive, the leader or chief responsible for co-ordinating the activities of the group, i.e. the head of the organization, tended to be looked upon also as the principle of fellowship as well. He was vested with

to represent God if they are, deliberately and socially, to relate themselves to Him and in that relationship establish themselves as a community of persons. But they must also constantly move beyond their representations if their relationship to God and to one another is not to be falsified.

religious symbols; he was the bearer of religious authority. The two unities, organic and personal, were confused in principle. Thus it was that every aspect of organized civic life had religious overtones.

But if, in the course of time, these elements have been separated out, the interpretation placed on the separation is not always adequate or happy. The emergence of purely secular society, whose authority or principle of unity is stripped of all divine attributes, has been thought of as leaving religion with nothing to do. Because God is not required for the organic constitution of the group, He is not, it is thought, required at all. Such an interpretation would be valid only if the only unity men needed in order to be and function as persons were the unity of an organization. That such is not the case we have already shown. Far, then, from eliminating any place for God in man's life, the emergence of the secular has pointed out more clearly just what that place is. God is the ground of unity among persons as persons, and the celebration of that ground, which is at the same time the celebration of community, is required if the community of persons as persons is to be achieved.

All too often this further move has not
been made. The objective signs and symbols pointing to that Presence which ex-
ceeds the possibilities of direct conceptual
representation, begin to be taken as adequate representations of God Himself.
Man's attention, then, instead of being
directed to the hidden One who is the correlative constituent of selfhood and the
unifying principle of community, becomes
focused on idols. What was present, but
hidden, becomes absent as well. God becomes a particular being to be served in
particular ways, and it is this particularism which then divides men from one another.

If this is the case, however, the problem of achieving community cannot be
solved by eliminating God or such ac-
knowledgement as there is of Him. In particular, the community of persons will not
be realized by following an ideal of this-
worldly humanism. So long as humanistic
aspirations are conceived as the product
of an individual's own mind and heart, ad-
herence to them, while it may engender a

true service of others and contribute to the improvement of man's lot (which is no small thing), will not establish the individual in an actual relationship of community with others. He will remain an individual following his own bent, however noble. Through lack of shared responsiveness to a universal Other, he will never feel himself caught up in an all-encompassing love nor have the redeeming awareness of actual fellowship. If, as Macmurray remarks, the function peculiar to religion is "to create, maintain and deepen the community of persons and to extend it without limit,"[41] the suppression of religion does more than wipe out its past shortcomings; it makes genuine human community impossible.

Since the human reaches fulfillment in the community of persons, the considerations we have so far developed indicate, I think, the primary bearing of God on human affairs. Since, on the other hand, God is able to unify the human community

41. *Persons in Relation,* p. 163.

only because He is the universal Other for each of us taken singly, attention to Him or the lack of it has also a profound bearing on the quality of our individual lives. Let me indicate briefly, therefore, three ways in which I think this is so. My contention will be that only an individual's awareness of and responsiveness to God allows him to achieve in his own life a sense of wholeness, identity and of final import.

For my life to have the quality of wholeness and coherence, there must be a way of binding together all the various responsibilities that define me at a given moment, as well as all the various episodes in which I am successively an actor. Since the self is correlative to the other, the self can be one only if the other is one. But the other in its immediacy is anything but one. It breaks down into a plurality of individuals, institutions, and systems each of which is continually making demands upon me. I have public responsibilities and private responsibilities, personal responsibilities and professional responsibilities. What is it that ties all these together? So long as they remain irreducibly many, my life is inevitably fragmented, compartmentalized. But suppose, as we have supposed, that my selfhood is constituted by a relation of responsibility towards a Transcendent Other whose intention must be met in all the situations of my life. If that is the case, everything is transformed. ". . . I am one within myself as I encounter the One in all that acts upon me."[42] When my world is divided, I am divided. But when everything is viewed in its bearing on the accomplishment of Your will, the achievement of community, then the world has a focus and I am one. My response to every particular action takes the form of a response to You. And since no matter where I go I am never out of Your presence, the successive phases of my life likewise cease to be disconnected episodes. Instead, they take on the structure of a continuing and developing encounter. It is thus my relation to God that enables me, as nothing

42. H. Richard Niebuhr, *The Responsible Self* (New York: Harper & Row, 1963), p. 122.

else can, to conceive my life simultaneously and successively as constituting a
single whole.

By the same token, it is also God Who
gives me my identity as a person. One of
the troubling features of our times is that
people in general seem to have lost the
sense of any defining and constitutive relationships. Whereas in the past, the institutions to which they belonged and in
which they participated gave them a sense
of identity, the general questioning of institutions prevalent today has left them
without this support. They literally do not
know who they are or what they are called
upon to do. Nor can they ever know so
long as God is forgotten. If beyond the
structures and patterns which are today
called into question there is nothing at all,
then the self is inevitably uprooted and
lost. But if beyond the changing patterns
it is You who call to me, then I have a
defining vocation and identity no matter
how fluid and transitory my surroundings.
I am Your agent and servant, called with
all men to promote Your reign in all that

I do. Thus just as You make my life whole,
You also give me back to myself.

Moreover, it is as an answer to You that
each of my actions has an import it would
otherwise lack. Arising from contemporary
man's grasp of the tremendous sweep of
time and from his new sense of himself
as involved in a creative process that opens
out endlessly into the future, there is a
gnawing feeling abroad that the individual and his actions are without any final
significance. If everything is in transition,
are not all my efforts doomed to be swept
aside in the creative advance of life? If
any particular deed is but an infinitesimal
dot on the endless line of becoming, a process whose goal I shall never know, then
what real difference does it make? Without God, the answer is clear: not very
much. But if in the present deed I stand
before the Transcendent and say Yes or
No to Him, then however slight the mark
of my deeds on the course of history, they
each bear the absolute weight of acceptance or rejection of God. If they are deeds
of love, so that He has a part in them, then

this gives them a substance which outweighs their effects. As responsive to His presence, they are more than merely contributory to the on-rushing course of events. They also have in themselves a kind of final and ultimate worth.

Finally, what about God and progress? What is the bearing of belief in God on man's vocation to share in the world's making? For religion has often been charged with being, and historically has often been, a rigidly conservative force bent on maintaining the *status quo*. Does not the centering of a person's life on a focus outside of time inevitably distract him from the work at hand and lead him to minimize temporal concerns? The answer, of course, depends on how our relationship to God is understood. If our relationship to God were something distinct from and independent of our relationship to the things and people who surround us, then the objection would have force. But if this relationship is one with our vocation to community, then a love for God cannot be realized as something in itself but only as qualifying all our particular relationships.[43] The reality of our responsiveness to God will be the humanity of our dealings with one another. It is only as working always for a fuller realization of the ideal of community that we are truly responsive to Him. Far, then, from restricting us to the actual shape of things, God's presence in our life is what continually calls us to move beyond where we are. We cannot rest until we have done all that we can to make love prevail in our world.

God, then, is not irrelevant, however much our images of Him may be. Nor is belief in Him, properly conceived, without positive bearing on the quality of our lives. In this last section, we have tried to sketch the kind of humanness belief alone makes possible. We might sum it up this way.

43.   Harvey Cox asserts: "God wants man to be interested not in Him but in his fellow man" (*The Secular City*, p. 265). Perhaps it is better to say, as we have, that God is interested in our relationship to Him, not as something separate and distinct, but as modifying all our relationships.

Eliminating the idea of God does not diminish His constitutive presence nor efface the effect of that presence in us, our native humanity. It simply precludes human wholeness and compels us to settle for less. But why settle for less?

The Aquinas Lectures

Published by the Marquette University Press
Milwaukee, Wisconsin 53233

Cicero in the Courtroom of St. Thomas Aquinas (1945) by E. K. Rand, Ph.D., Litt.D., LL.D., (1871-1945) Pope professor of Latin, *emeritus*, Harvard University.

St. Thomas and Epistemology (1946) by Louis-Marie Regis, O.P., Th.L., Ph.D., director of the Albert the Great Institute of Mediaeval Studies, University of Montreal.

St. Thomas and the Greek Moralists (1947, Spring) by Vernon J. Bourke, Ph.D., professor of philosophy, St. Louis University, St. Louis, Missouri.

History of Philosophy and Philosophical Education (1947, Fall) by Étienne Gilson of the *Académie française*, director of studies and professor of the history of Mediaeval philosophy, Pontifical Institute of Mediaeval Studies, Toronto.

The Natural Desire for God (1948) by William R. O'Connor, S.T.L., Ph.D., former professor of dogmatic theology, St. Joseph's Seminary, Dunwoodie, N.Y.

St. Thomas and the World State (1949) by Robert M. Hutchins, former Chancellor of the University of Chicago, president of the Fund for the Republic.

Method in Metaphysics (1950) by Robert J. Henle, S.J., Ph.D., academic vice-president, St. Louis University, St. Louis, Missouri.

Wisdom and Love in St. Thomas Aquinas (1951) by Étienne Gilson of the *Académie française*, director of studies and professor of the history of Mediaeval philosophy, Pontifical Institute of Mediaeval Studies, Toronto.

The Good in Existential Metaphysics (1952) by Elizabeth G. Salmon, Ph.D., professor of philosophy in the graduate school, Fordham University.

St. Thomas and the Object of Geometry (1953) by Vincent Edward Smith, Ph.D., director, Philosophy of Science Institute, St. John's University.

Realism and Nominalism Revisited (1954) by Henry Veatch, Ph.D., professor and chairman of the department of philosophy, Northwestern University.

Imprudence in St. Thomas Aquinas (1955) by Charles J. O'Neil, Ph.D., professor of philosophy, Villanova University.

The Truth That Frees (1956) by Gerard Smith, S.J., Ph.D., professor and chairman of the department of philosophy, Marquette University.

St. Thomas and the Future of Metaphysics (1957) by Joseph Owens, C.Ss.R., Ph.D., professor of philosophy, Pontifical Institute of Mediaeval Studies, Toronto.

Thomas and the Physics of 1958: A Confrontation (1958) by Henry Margenau, Ph.D.,

Eugene Higgins professor of physics and natural philosophy, Yale University.

Metaphysics and Ideology (1959) by Wm. Oliver Martin, Ph.D., professor of philosophy, University of Rhode Island.

Language, Truth and Poetry (1960) by Victor M. Hamm, Ph.D., professor of English, Marquette University.

Metaphysics and Historicity (1961) by Emil L. Fackenheim, Ph.D., professor of philosophy, University of Toronto.

The Lure of Wisdom (1962) by James D. Collins, Ph.D., professor of philosophy, St. Louis University.

Religion and Art (1963) by Paul Weiss, Ph.D. Sterling professor of philosophy, Yale University.

St. Thomas and Philosophy (1964) by Anton C. Pegis, Ph.D., professor of philosophy, Pontifical Institute of Mediaeval Studies, Toronto.

The University In Process (1965) by John O. Riedl, Ph.D., professor of philosophy, Marquette University.

The Pragmatic Meaning of God (1966) by Robert O. Johann, S.J., associate professor of philosophy, Fordham University.

Uniform format, cover and binding.